POETIC RESPONSES TO THE EFFECTS OF EPILEPSY

poems by

Edward P. McMorrow

Finishing Line Press
Georgetown, Kentucky

POETIC RESPONSES TO THE EFFECTS OF EPILEPSY

*Dedicated with gratitude to my parents and life-long caregivers,
Mr. Philip E. McMorrow and Ms. Isabel S. McMorrow*

Copyright © 2016 by Edward P. McMorrow
ISBN 978-1-944899-02-8 First Edition
All rights reserved under International and Pan-American Copyright Conventions. No part of this book may be reproduced in any manner whatsoever without written permission from the publisher, except in the case of brief quotations embodied in critical articles and reviews.

ACKNOWLEDGMENTS

"FURTHER CONFINEMENT" was included in *From the Storm, Artists with Temporal Lobe Epilepsy*, created by Jennifer Hall, Do While Studio, Boston, MA., November 1993, and in *2014 Hidden Truths, The Mind Unraveled* sponsored by the Epilepsy Foundation of America and Epilepsy Therapy Project.

"THE SEIZURAPIDS" was included as "THE RAPIDS" in *2014 Hidden Truths, The Mind Unraveled* sponsored by the Epilepsy Foundation of America and Epilepsy Therapy Project.

"THE LIGHT AT THE END OF THE TUNNEL" was included in *2014 Hidden Truths, The Mind Unraveled* sponsored by the Epilepsy Foundation of America and Epilepsy Therapy Project.

"THE RIVER" (p.20) was also included in the exhibit, *From the Storm: Artists With Temporal Lobe Epilepsy*, shown in November 1993.

Editor: Christen Kincaid

Author Photo: Nancy Coffey

Cover Design: Elizabeth Maines

Printed in the USA on acid-free paper.
Order online: www.finishinglinepress.com
also available on amazon.com

Author inquiries and mail orders:
Finishing Line Press
P. O. Box 1626
Georgetown, Kentucky 40324
U. S. A.

Table of Contents

I. MY LIFE IS LIKE A WIDE, TREACHEROUSLY INHOSPITABLE, INESCAPABLE LAND

The Wasteland 1
Tides 2
The Lighthouse 3
Lost in the Darkness 4
Someday 5
The Road Ahead 6
The Lonely Maze 8
The Clearing 9

II. DREAMS OF FREEDOM

The Past Has Passed 12
Waiting 13
Super Patient 14
Dreaming 15
My Yearning 16
Independence Day 17
The Glowing Ray of Hope 18

III. SWEPT INEXORABLY DOWNSTREAM BY THE TORRENTIAL FLOOD OF SEIZURES

The River 20
The Seizurapids 22
The Light at the End of the Tunnel 23

IV. LOVE AND FRIENDSHIP

My Lost Friend 26
Enlightened by Love 28
The Birthday Present 29
Sailing Together 30
Someday With Friends 32

V. DIRECT REFERENCES TO EPILEPSY

Further Confinement 34
The Questions 35
Lonely 36

VI. IN CONTEMPT FOR THOSE WHO ABANDON THEIR GOOD HEALTH AND WALK INTO THEIR OWN ENDLESS TUNNEL OF DARKNESS FOR A HIGH:

The Waste of Our Most Precious Resource 38

I.

MY LIFE IS LIKE A WIDE, TREACHEROUSLY INHOSPITABLE, INESCAPABLE LAND

THE WASTELAND

Originally written shortly after learning that I was experiencing seizures due to epilepsy which had been misdiagnosed but prevented by medication and a careful diet for around ten years.

Astray and wandering on the wide plain of smooth sterile snow.
And unable to hear any more than the cold winds eerily blow,
Polishing the smoothly barren Siberian steppe in their flight
Bleached white, reflecting all the unimpeded sunlight.

The sun glares from the clear icy blue heaven
No longer generating warmth as the stellar oven
Only bright light reflected by the mirror-like snow
Isolated by frigid weather as the chilling winds blow.

Its intensity amplifying the chaos in the brain,
This reflected glare has nearly blinded the eyes in pain
Already of little use adrift on the reflectively smooth sea
Of nothing but featureless white snow for anyone to see.

Wandering in seclusion around this cloister of desolation,
No companions inhabit this monastery of frustration
Doomed to inevitable loneliness having lost my way in the cold.
I wish to meet someone willing to warm me, by being bold.

Instead, an icy blizzard of hatred swirls all around me,
Doomed to endure such harshly icy enmity helplessly.
These unforgiving surroundings seem inconsiderate,
Lacking any kindly sign of a willingness to exonerate.

Disoriented and restricted inescapably
By my inherent, neurological disability,
I have been exiled to, and left wandering
On this wasteland of frustrated stumbling.

There is so little that I can do now or believe
That I will ever improve, enabling me to achieve.

TIDES

Originally written the night before moving into the apartment where I would live while a graduate student at Boston College. Dedicated to Steve and Francesca Barry, my landlords, in gratitude for their help and support.

I am adrift and alone
At the mercy of all
The forces which beset me,
Like wind and wave and tide.

I must go where I am taken,
Without any way to determine
Either my eventual destination,
Or my ultimate foe.

Slowly I am drawn
Inexorably out to sea.
Steadily the familiar shore fades
As I approach the stark, unknown horizon.

This world is neither as I would choose,
Nor is my life my own.
I can change nothing,
For I am trapped and confined.

Without any control over my course,
I am hopelessly lost and helplessly
Lonely for any recipient
Of my calls for help.

THE LIGHTHOUSE

> *Originally written for Shawna Line, a Gordon College student whom I saw periodically when she came to help Mom with household tasks once a week.*

Abandoned and adrift in the cold and
Darkness of the wide, open sea of my world,
I have despaired from loneliness,
Almost losing all my hope of relief.

Now, in the distance I can see a dim beacon
Toward which finally I can steer, enabling me,
Apparently, to gradually regain control of the
Drifting, storm-battered, leaky hulk of my life.

It is a difficult, time-consuming task.
My progress seems painfully slow,
And often retrograde and off course.
Causing my fragile hope to waver.

Through it all, you are still there, though
Not beside me, as I would like, for I love you,
But close enough that your regular visits
Provide the warmth and the light for my goal.

LOST IN THE DARKNESS

> *Originally written in reaction to the failure of my April 1985 brain surgery, which had seemed to stop my seizures for about one year until I began experiencing them once again, in May, 1986, about one month after the first anniversary, of the unsuccessful operation.*

Apparently, the long, dark journey had ended,
For months, I seemed to have finally reached
My destination and emerged, then bathed in,
The warm glow of the light at the end of the tunnel.

Suddenly, the truth had been revealed.
As I find myself still lost in the onerous funnel,
As it extends and continues onward
Endlessly into the darkness.

As the deep shadowy gloom thickens again,
The escape to which I aspire perpetually retreats.
As all hope of reaching any such distant light
Grows forever more remote.

SOMEDAY

Here I stand,
Lost in the middle of the wide, trackless plain.
My goal is over the horizon,
And I know not how to reach it.

I am restricted and confined
By the inherent limitations of my person,
And, the environment's response
To those restrictions.

Here I stand,
Lost in thought,
As I attempt to deal with my confinement,
And to reach my goal.

I have found friends
Who have helped me
To attempt to overcome the restraints,
And to search for my goal.

Perhaps, with their helpless
And with much thought and effort,
I will overcome my inherent inhibitions,
And achieve my goal, someday.

THE ROAD AHEAD

Originally "Graduation," 4/21/84, one month before receiving my undergraduate degree from Tufts University,

My life, the road into the future, wander
Endlessly onward, never reassuringly straight,
Towards one, discernibly particular destination
In one comprehensibly definite direction.

Instead, my thoroughfare is ominously dark, overcast, and
Obscured by opaquely dense pea-soup fog, with a
Rough, gravelly, pot-holed pavement, painful to cross,
Rather than a smoothly unstained surface of yellow brick.

For so long, insecurely confused and uncertain,
I have been obsessed with reaching that next bend in the road,
In the hope that my strenuously sought destination,
The "Emerald City" lies just beyond.

But, having reached this curve, I am hesitant now
To actually continue around it, at the risk of again finding nothing
But a dim, murky, further continuation of my interminably painful trek
Confirming the apparent futility of my efforts, and struggle onward.

For so many years,
My immediate future seemed secure.
While the road ahead was apparently endless,
There were no obstacles or sharp corners.

My goals always seem to shimmer ahead,
Never entirely attainable,

But forever my raison d'etre,
A fixture in my life.

Some goals have been achieved,
Upon reaching each bend in the road.
Yet now I am stalled in the dark
And perplexed as to what to do

There is so little that I can do now or believe
That I will ever improve, enabling me to achieve.
Some accomplishment of great importance
Am I to be forever doomed to insignificance?

THE LONELY MAZE

> *Originally written in readiness for earning my Master of Arts from Boston College, and unsure about my future, whether to seek employment and maintain it if possible, or take the chance of working academically toward a PhD. Also considering any possibility of both my living on my own and my ever finding a wife, both fruitless ever since.*

My life is like an endlessly vast maze, constantly expanding
And complicating, so that dozens of seizures seem to occur
Revealing new pathways and obstacles whenever it seems
That the long sought goal of my quest finally grows near.

I am alone, as I wander through the lonely labyrinth.
Desperate for support and guidance, I must helplessly
Endure all the trials of my arduously endless journey,
Lacking any companion with whom I can share the ordeal.

Perhaps, someday, somewhere, I will
Encounter such a friend and, with her assistance,
I will reach the exit from the maze, to my goals,
Freedom from my epilepsy, and from my loneliness.

I can only hope that, on some amazing day,
My path will suddenly become smooth, straight,
And clear of both barriers and detours,
Enabling my dreams to come true.

THE CLEARING

> *Original version written 8/30/93 after I began to feel much better by escaping from the side effects of the study drug, Vigabatrin, after a dose reduction.*

Perpetually lost at sea, amidst a thick, pea soup fog,
Violently thrown by towering, crashing waves and
Swept by cold, swirling wind and hard, driving rain
In darkness, I have been impenetrable to any hope.

Now, after such a seemingly endless time of oblivion,
The storm winds have begun to quiet and abate,
Allowing the waves to diminish and gradually calm,
The fog to rapidly clear, and the sunlight to return.

Still buffeted by the rough, choppy seas,
I am not yet able to resume my course for landfall.
Though, finally I can faintly perceive it now,
There, on the horizon, through the waning rain,

And there, in the distance, I know,
Lies that safe harbor, my ultimate goal.
Accessible once the seas have calmed,
The winds have stilled, and the air has cleared.

Regaining control of my course, after riding out the storm,
I will then resume my voyage into the future.

II. DREAMS OF FREEDOM

THE PAST HAS PASSED

About so much, there is nothing we can do.
        Including many things which cause us pain.
Despite everything that makes one feel blue,
        Remember that for each loss there is a gain,
And with each bad side comes a good side, too.

Que era', era', what has been, has been.
        Although sometimes one might wonder why,
We cannot change what happened way back when,
        Or the deeds of people from days gone by,
Echoing in our lives still, every now and then.

Que sera', sera'; around us, what will be, will be.
        We are helpless to control or alter,
So many events which we will never see,
        And the actions of those many other
Which will affect the lives of you and me.

For what is not owned, we must not be obsessed
        Or mourn for all that we cannot do.
One must be content with what is possessed,
        And recall that we are very lucky, too,
To have those skills with which we are blessed.

WAITING

Original version written shortly before undergoing brain surgery in April, 1985 (at age 23!), in the Boston Children's Hospital. Although apparently successful initially, the operation was ultimately ineffective

Here I am, nervously waiting,
In suspense for Friday,
For the day after tomorrow,
The date of the surgery.

Apprehensively, I await the operation
Which, we hope, will correct the basic,
Original problem, and thereby put an end
To my repetitive epileptic seizures.

If the surgeons can achieve this,
And terminate my frequent seizures,
Finally I will have been unshackled from the
Chains which have confined burdened me.

I would be liberated and free to go forth
Into the great wide world, unrestricted, and
Ultimately able to fulfill so many of my dreams
And possibly those of others, as well.

SUPER PATIENT

> *Written while undergoing a long term EEG (ElectroEncephaloGram) test in which electrodes attached to my scalp detect electric activity within my brain for analysis of my epilepsy symptoms.*

The patient is helplessly lying there, all alone,
Patiently enduring a dully throbbing, relentless pain,
And other irritating discomforts without a groan,
Shackled to that wretched bed, where so long he has lain.

While entangled in a spider's web of electrodes, by the doctors' whims
Pasted to his head, to monitor the ceaseless activity of his brain.
In addition to multiple catheters injected painfully into all his limbs.
Pumping unknown liquids into him, who is ignorant of what they contain.

Tirelessly, I am laboring to endure this ordeal, resolutely refusing to fall,
A tranquilly forbearing patient, imagining myself a super-hero who will find
That I can achieve the power and ability to fly clear of the hospi-tall
Buildings imprisoning me in a single leap of my patiently hopeful mind.

DREAMING

Here I sit, dreaming of ideal things,
In the greater world around me.
Such as a dream of peace, the absence of war.
How much I wish that they would be.

I dream of a world in which everyone works together,
Toward the greater good welfare of us all,
Rather than death and destruction
As a means to achieve their selfish goals.

I dream of ideal things in my world, too.
Such as a dream of health, and freedom
From the neurological malfunctions which restrict me,
Freedom to live a normal, adult life.

I dream of ideal, impractical things,
For myself, as well as for the world around me.
How much I wish that they could be.
Here I sit, endlessly dreaming.

MY YEARNING:

Somehow, Someday, Somewhere, Someone, Something?

Someday I will be unshackled from these
Chains which have always confined me
And prevented us from achieving so much
Of which we would otherwise be capable.

Someday I will escape to freedom, having been
Released, enabling me to accomplish so much with
The liberty to go out, and both to work towards my
Long dormant ambitions and to attain our dreams.

Somewhere I will go, where I can work to resolve
An age-old dilemma, finally able to seek fulfillment
Having traveled all over the world, while seeing so
Many places and meeting so many people.

Someone of them will be a lovely lady who will love me
And willingly marry me, despite my imperfections, as
Well as encourage and cherish me, as I will cherish her
While we live the rest of our lives together, in happiness.

Something, of which I have always dreamed, I will do, because
The solution of those enigmatic problems will be an opportunity
For truly great achievement, when enhancing my own world will
Ultimately enable me to improve our world in general, somehow.

INDEPENDENCE DAY

Originally written one day after returning from long term EEG analysis of epilepsy symptoms at Massachusetts General Hospital.

Finally, I am home, on the fourth of July.
I have awoken here, in my own soft bed,
Free of all the wires in which I was forced to lie,
Feeding the EEG by being attached to my head,
And restricting me for almost a week gone by

Having been able to eat my regular breakfast,
Finally now, I can go to shave and shower.
In that soft, warm, deluge, in which I can rest
And use that shampoo, the cleaning power
Of which I had dreamed during the entire test.

Realizing the meaning of this anniversary, I can say
That my freedom now is both appropriate and ironic.
My first day to appreciate these things more than play
And do much more than watching fireworks iconic …
After so many years, this is my own Independence Day

THE GLOWING RAY OF HOPE

Originally inspired by receiving an Easter card from Keiko, my Japanese email pal, and a letter from Shawna while I was undergoing a Long Term Monitoring EEG test in Boston Children's Hospital, two years after my unsuccessful brain surgery there

Everything is gloomy.
Densely dark clouds
Are looming
Ominously low over me.

Nowhere is there light.
I am surrounded,
Confined, and constricted,
Swallowed by darkness.

Suddenly, an irresistibly strong beam
Of intensely bright light penetrates
Those deep thick shadows, thereby
Restoring my sight and my hope.

Implausibly, this fortuitously warm light beam,
Has radiated from welcome mail sent by friends,
Whose beautiful faces I have not seen in weeks.
Miraculously warming and brightening my life,

III. SWEPT INEXORABLY DOWNSTREAM BY THE TORRENTIAL FLOOD OF SEIZURES

THE RIVER

> *Incorporated in "From the Storm, Artists with Temporal Lobe Epilepsy" Created by Jennifer Hall, Do While Studio, Boston, MA. November 1993*

Gradually I have been dragged along,
By the relentless waters.
The rushing sound
Is always in my ears.

Toward an unseen destination,
I am swept.
The rushing sound
Is always in my ears.

I am not free to alter my course
I go where the river takes me.
The rushing sound
Is always in my ears.

Many calm, serene pools are passed by.
But I cannot stop and rest.
The rushing sound
Is always in my ears.

In the distance, obscured to sight
Is the river's mouth.
The rushing sound
Is always my ears.

Here I stand,
Lost in the middle of the wide, trackless plain.
My goal is over the horizon,
And I know not how to reach it.

I am restricted and confined
By the inherent limitations of my person
And by the environment's response
To those limitations.

Here I stand,
Lost in thought,
As I attempt to deal with my limitations
And to reach my goal.

I have found friends
Who have helped me
To attempt to overcome the limitations
And to search for my goal.

Perhaps, with their help
And with much thought and effort,
I will overcome my inherent limitations
And achieve my goal, someday.

THE SEIZURAPIDS

My voyage down the river of life, often gray and slow,
At times seemingly through an unchanging landscape, is
Long and tedious, without hope to find anything of value.
Instead, around the next bend I will encounter an ordeal.

Suddenly, without warning, I encounter a stretch of rapids,
Throwing me swiftly over a perilously rocky, shallow riverbed.
Helpless, I am tumbling out of control, swept relentlessly
By the ceaselessly torrential, deafening, cascade of the waters

Unable to decelerate, I lose all awareness and coherence of
The chaos through which I am passing as well as all that I am
Doing in response to my plight in this situation. Leaving me
With no concept of either my plight or my situation.

Incarcerated by the river's flow, even beyond the rapids, I am
Frustrated by my capability to neither control my course, nor
Pause and rest, sheltered from the torrential gush of the river,
In any peacefully placid pools, which rush enticingly passed.

Far ahead of me, I hope, lies a port, safe and secure,
Offering relief from my tempestuous, often violent, voyage.
Yet, I wonder both at the existence of such a place, and at
My own ability to escape to it from the drag of the strong current.

THE LIGHT AT THE END OF THE TUNNEL

> *Begun after new dose of medications seemed to be making great progress in controlling seizures*

For so long, he had dragged himself upstream so far
Lost in the darkness of the endless, narrow, rocky tunnel.
Through the torrential flow of the icy river water
Gushing from the conduit ahead as if it were a funnel

Always fighting against the force of that strongly pulling current, even
When it was accelerated by those periodically devastating rapids,
He held on by resolutely grasping those slippery fragments of wet stone
Of the rocky stream bed with his stiffly frozen hands

Suddenly, ahead he noticed feebly tiny bits of light flashing
Through the seemingly impenetrable obscurity of the dim
Darkness after reflecting from the cold waters rushing
Towards him while he was wearily crawling into them.

The weak light flickered from the tunnel's distant end.
From a great distance it had appeared, apparently
Far ahead upstream, after he had rounded the last bend,
Over the calmer waters now flowing more gently.

Tenaciously he heaved himself forward over the stream bed
Determined to overcome the force of the maelstrom
To continue his difficult progress toward those bits of light ahead
By extricating himself from that counteractive inundation

Having pledged neither to abandon his endlessly tiresome trek
To reach that warm daylight flickering through the obscurity from so far
Nor to abandon ship because his journey made him felt like such a wreck
That he could not stay afloat any longer and must founder.

As he slowly neared the departure the light was growing
More vividly as he approached the cavern mouth
Into which the stream had long been flowing.
Beneath the thick labyrinth of the overgrowth

Strongly encouraged, he has preserved the full measure
Of his determination to maintain his tireless tenacity
And never forsake his indefatigable quest for that treasure
Which would improve his life with such immensity

Finally, he emerges into the glow of warm sunlight
Which had inspired him by reflecting from the stream
Now he feels so much warmer and relaxed and bright
Having finally arrived in the land of his dreams

IV. LOVE AND FRIENDSHIP

MY LOST FRIEND

In memory of Kimmy, my fellow five year old childhood friend and hospital patient dying of leukemia, forty-eight years ago.

I

There I was, once again, a little boy in a hospital bed,
Surrounded by intimidating women in snowy white.
Although armed with sharp little needles, they said
That nothing really hurt while I writhed from their bite

Harshly cold like the winds of a blizzard, they blasted me,
While subjecting me to so many arduously painful diagnoses
Even then, after a variety of difficult tasks, I was not free
From their penalties for my disrespect or malfeasances.

In a nearby bed, you were also there, terminally ill and lonely.
A sweet little girl, stoically enduring a similarly painful situation
While thirsting for some friendly bedside reading, as if only
Freezing and alone amid the silently white polar desolation.

For your rescue and relief, you needed both a reader and a friend
There I was, an equally small but literate child, in my adjacent bed,
Who became your pal, able to read your books beginning to end,
Enabling us to escape into the fantasy of your books as I read.

II

One morning, I awoke to find that your bed was empty!
Shocked and bewildered, I wondered where could you have gone?
After my quick look 'round for you, and confused by its futility,
I wandered apprehensively barefoot to the nurse's station.

To inquire where you could be, or at what place might you be spied?
In response, after that woman in white looked at me quizzically,
She casually inquired in reply, hadn't I heard that you had died?
Her shocking words came with a crushing impact, devastating me.

So many years later, that cataclysmic news of your demise,
A crushing jolt when learned, remains my first, most painful memory,
A question still torments me, after that dreadful surprise
What might you have become, if you had grown up like me?

You were forcibly abducted from me and those others around you.
Unlike those other girlfriends who have chosen to reject me since.
If not, could we still be friends now, or perhaps even wedded, too?
For you were more beloved than those others who made me wince.

III
In my dreams, you are now the lady dressed in warm ivory
Coming serenely down the aisle on the arm of your father.
Nervously standing at the altar, I await you eagerly.
A lovely lady in white approaching who would not scare.

I treasure this image of you, resurrected, returning to me.
We are listening to the priest reading to the congregation,
Together on the threshold of nirvana awaiting the key
As you had listened to my reading from others' imagination

Then we would enter the idyllic bridal suite together
Hand in hand, unlike meeting in that cold hospital ward.,
We would be warmly, affectionately holding each other
Far more comfortable in one imaginary, luxuriously large bed,

What an ideal remedy this could be, bringing rejuvenation
For us both, the unquestionably effective cure for all our ills.
Then, having achieved complete recovery and recuperation,
We could rehabilitate together, finally free from taking pills.

ENLIGHTENED BY LOVE

> *Written while undergoing Long Term EEG Monitoring at Children's Hospital and having just received mail and Easter gifts from Keiko Sakai and Shawna Line.*

The clouds looming above us
Are thick, dark, and threatening.
Leaving no light anywhere, and
Only a gloomy world around us.

Tonight, I am even more confined than usual, connected
To the monitoring machine by a tangled web of wires
Linked to my head and other points on my body, and
Preventing my leaving the hospital bed.

Suddenly, the thoughts and care of sweet, lovely friends
Have arrived like a ray of strong light slicing through the
Darkness and enabling me to see that there is hope.
This sudden light has illuminated my day.

THE BIRTHDAY PRESENT

Original version written after receiving birthday gift, card, and letter from Keiko at her college, North Texas State University.

I am beset, as if by a storm, as piercing winds of
Uncertainty swirl around me, beneath heavy clouds of
Melancholy looming above, and pouring forth icy rains
Soaking into, and leaving, my thoughts chilled and cold.

Suddenly, the rains abates, and the clouds break.
The sun is revealed, clearing my mind with sunlight.
The harsh winds of my confusion gradually decrease, for
A beloved friend has remembered me, bringing change

SAILING TOGETHER

Originally written inspired by my acceptance as a volunteer in the Beverly Hospital Pharmacy and at a restaurant party for the resignation of a pharmacist, and friend, Dick Banville. Dedicated to him, Pharmacy liaison Ida Beaver, and all my other friends there,

I

During the long, endlessly lonely voyage of my life,
I have been swept endlessly across that vast open sea,
Dragged first to ascend the towering waves, and then,
Dropped into the precipitous troughs between them,

My ability to maintain my course has been
Limited by the whimsy of wind and wave.
I can only sail where propelled by the randomly
Strong breeze, or float aimlessly when becalmed.

I have frequently been seized by the cold, unexpected,
Violently stormy effects of my mental idiosyncrasies, often
Causing the icy tiller, and my control, to slip from my grasp,
Leaving me helplessly adrift with the flow of the waves.

II

At last, I have been directed to a convoy
Of fellow sailors who have accepted me,
Despite my unsteady grip on the steering wheel,
And guided me when I have gone adrift.

Having been accepted into this community,
My voyage has now grown easier.
Everyone sails together cooperatively,
Able to rely on each other in time of need.

Finally, we have reached a sheltered bay,
And anchored together in the safe harbor.
Though a stranger accepted en route,
I am now able to anchor in a berth with the others.

SOMEDAY, WITH FRIENDS

For all my friends at the Beverly Hospital Pharmacy and Volunteer Office, 1989–2009

Here I stand, lost in the midst
Of a wide, barren, and trackless plain.
My goal is beyond the horizon
And I do not know how to reach it.

Despite the unobstructed landscape,
I am restricted and confined
By my inherent limitations,
And the world's response to them.

Lost in thought, as well as
In orientation, course, and pace,
I attempt to overcome those obstacles,
Standing in the road to my goal.

Thankfully, I have found loyal, stalwart friends
Who have tirelessly helped me to battle both
My imperfections and the scorn of so many others
While searching for the route to my goal.

Perhaps, with their strong, ceaseless assistance,
And so much helpful effort and support from them,
I will overcome my impediments,
Enabling me to achieve my goal, someday.

V. DIRECT REFERENCES TO EPILEPSY

FURTHER CONFINEMENT

> *While hospitalized undergoing long term EEG and then transmitted for the several days of the long term test to an information receiver.*

I am confined.
The wires are attached to my head;
They monitor my brain waves
Then transmit them to the recording device.

I must keep the wires in place;
I must not go beyond the range of the transmitter.
I am confined.

I must remain so until I have had several seizures.
Now, when I want them, I have none.
Thus, I am more confined than usual,
And have less control ever over my life.

THE QUESTIONS

What can I do? What shall I do?
What is there for me to do?

These are the questions which haunt me,
As I sit here, confined to me cell and
Feeling helpless and impotent.

Near and far, the world rushes around me,
As so many people do so much
That I can see, hear, or only learn of.

When can I ever use my educations, my skills?
Having cherished them for so long,
Will I ever be able to achieve my goals?

LONELY

Here I sit
Confined by epilepsy
Kept from life
And alone.

I ache to pursue the dreams
That fill my mind,
Prevented by the seizures
That twist my brain.

I am taken aback as I see
My baby sisters growing up
And out into the adult world.
Leaving me behind.

I wish for a friend,
With whom I could share
My thoughts, my love,
My life.

I attempt, yet fail
To reach out to such a friend.
My reach is restricted
As is the rest of my life.

I sit and watch
As the world goes by,
Leaving me still
In its wake.

VI. IN SYMPATHY FOR THOSE WHO ABANDON THEIR GOOD HEALTH AND WALK INTO THEIR OWN ENDLESS TUNNEL FOR A HIGH

THE WASTE OF OUR MOST PRECIOUS RESOURCE

Some of those in perfectly good health, are carelessly seeking gratification in addictive substance abuse, willfully discarding their perfect health, an advantage which they were so fortunate to possess, unlike myself and so many others

I

Daily born, most infants are healthy, auspiciously
Beginning their lives and development from infancy
Into childhood while learning to use their abilities,
Enabling them to mature like their contemporaries.

Unfortunately, some new babies are deficient somewhere
With some of their natural functions or abilities impaired
Without which they are required to live their lives often
Forced to bear the inextricable weight of another burden

But the majority live on naively, in implicitly good health
Free from all that has deprived us of that invaluable wealth
Sparking the frustration and envy of us unable to compare
To those unspoiled by the defects which have us impaired.

II

Not everyone born in good shape can stay that way
For that advantage could be lost to a mishap someday,
An illness or serious accident causing crippling harm
Impairing or taking a person's abilities, to his alarm.

Like that vastly pristine wilderness long inviolate
Before our farming for crops and resources despoiled it
Through drilling for petroleum, or blasting for coal,
Heedless of the natural damage done to reach our goals

But not all of those people, blooming like that unspoiled land,
Have wisdom to preserve their fitness and that where they stand
Instead they seek careless thrills, throwing away so much
Of their natural wellness like that of so many places treated such

III

Much natural and human well-being is wasted, not treasured
From unspoiled lands, clean air and so much else never measured
As well as that of addicts who have condemned themselves
By using needles, pills, alcohol, and cigarettes from their shelves.

Just as wells are drilled into lands to drain away their petroleum
Needles are stabbed into arms to feed addictive needs for opium
And like explosives are buried to blast away land for coal mines
Opiate pills are often taken that blow away the addicts' minds.

By carelessly wasting their once fine shape for suicidal thrills,
Criminal highs from their addictive taking of those harmful pills.
Losing a treasure for which we would give so much to find some day.
For our own precious health like that they have foolishly thrown away

www.ingramcontent.com/pod-product-compliance
Lightning Source LLC
Chambersburg PA
CBHW060223050426
42446CB00013B/3152